ROSE CREEK PUBLIC LIBRARY
4476 TOWNE LAKE PKWY.
WOODSTOCK, GA 30188

DYNASTIES

Jonathan Bliss

The Rourke Corporation, Inc.
Vero Beach, Florida 32964

Copyright 1992 by The Rourke Corporation, Inc.

All rights reserved. No part of this book may be reproduced or utilized in any form or by any means, electronic or mechanical, including photocopying, recording or by any information storage and retrieval system without permission in writing from the publisher.

The Rourke Corporation, Inc.
P.O. Box 3328, Vero Beach, FL 32964

Bliss, Jonathan.
    Dynasties / by Jonathan Bliss.
       p.   cm. — (Football heroes)
    Includes bibliographical references (p. 47) and index.
    Summary: Examines the few teams in professional football who consistently had championship seasons and excelled on the field.
    ISBN 0-86593-156-9
    1. Football—United States—Clubs—History—Juvenile literature. 2. Super Bowl (Game)—Juvenile literature. [1. Football—History.] I. Title. II. Series.
GV954.B55 1992
796.332'64'10973—dc20   92-412
                                                                                                                     CIP
                                                                                                                      AC

Series Editor: Gregory Lee
Editor: Marguerite Aronowitz
Book design and production: The Creative Spark, San Clemente, CA
Cover photograph: Jim Spoontz/ALLSPORT

Contents

The Halas Touch	5
Lombardi And The New AFL	13
From New York To Dallas	21
The Dolphins And The Steelers	29
Dynasties Of The Eighties	37
Stats	42
Glossary	45
Bibliography	47
Index	48

Vince Lombardi (left) and George Halas (right) both shaped great NFL dynasties, and are now enshrined in the Pro Football Hall of Fame.

The Halas Touch

Professional football may be the ultimate team sport. No other competition requires so much effort from so many. In other sports, like basketball and baseball, one or two great players can make the difference between a good team and a championship team. Add Michael Jordan and Scottie Pippen to the Chicago Bulls, for example, and the team has a championship season. Put Babe Ruth and Lou Gehrig together, and you have one of the greatest teams that ever played baseball.

In football, however, it always takes more than just a few star players to make a winning team. Many great athletes have labored long and hard on a losing team. Dan Fouts was a great quarterback, yet because he played on the defenseless San

---

Dynasty Trivia

Q: What NFL-NFC team has made the most championship game appearances?
A: The New York Giants, with 16.

Q: What AFL-AFC team has made the most championship game appearances?
A: The Oakland-L.A. Raiders, with 12.

Q: Name the only two NFL teams to win four Super Bowls.
A: The Pittsburgh Steelers (IX, X, XIII, XIV) and the San Francisco 49ers (XVI, XIX, XXIII, XXIV).

Diego Chargers, he had few opportunities to show his exceptional passing arm in post-season play. Steve Largent was one of the best wide receivers in NFL history, yet playing with the Seattle Seahawks made it difficult for him to even get to the post-season.

Great offense can't win without great defense, and great defense can't win without a potent offense. Without good special teams—like the kicking and return squads—an otherwise great team can't win consistently. And even the best-balanced squad has difficulty winning without a good coaching staff and supportive owner. No matter how good a quarterback, linebacker, tailback, or safety is, if he isn't surrounded by equally competent team members, the team doesn't have a chance.

This is why it is so difficult to establish a tradition of winning in the NFL, and why few coaches and general managers last very long. It's not enough to train a current roster of players, keep them healthy through a grueling 16-game schedule, and come up with the right play at the right time during a game. With 11 players on a field, there are 11 things that can go wrong on any individual play—too many ways in which a team can foul up. Is it any wonder then that there have been so many poor teams fielded in the NFL, and so few great teams?

Several teams in NFL history were almost great: for example, the Cleveland Browns, the Denver Broncos, and the Minnesota Vikings. These teams were always on the verge of great things. The Broncos lost the Super Bowl four times—three in the span of four years. The Vikings always had a great team that also finished second in the Super Bowl four times. Wonderful teams, but not *dynasties*—a team that is successful year after year.

This book discusses the few NFL teams that have won year after year, piling up championships. This is the story of dynasties.

Papa Bear

In the beginning, there was George Halas. Few people ever loved football the way George Halas loved it, and few people loved football as early as George Halas.

Born in 1895, George Halas attended the University of Illinois where he played both baseball and football. After graduation in 1918, he served in the U.S. Navy until the end of World War I, then played major league baseball with the New York Yankees. But after playing baseball for one year, he discovered that his first love was really football. Halas returned to Illinois, and in 1921 organized the Chicago Bears football team. Why did he do it? Certainly not to make money. Professional football was not a popular game in the early '20s. In fact, the few professional teams that existed played maybe five games a year. He was probably looking for an excuse to play, and decided the best way was by starting his own franchise.

By 1922 Halas had moved the team from Decatur, Illinois, to Chicago. Along the way he developed into a great defensive end, setting a pro football record that stood for many years: He returned a recovered fumble 98 yards for a touchdown. At the same time he was playing, Halas was also coaching his team—something no player would think of doing today.

As player, coach, and owner of the Bears, Halas changed the sport forever by signing Red Grange in 1925. Grange had gained the attention of the sporting public with his great speed and extraordinary ability to elude tacklers. When Halas signed Grange, the Chicago Bears instantly became popular. Thirty-six thousand people turned out to see Grange play his first game. One week later, 68,000 fans jammed the old Polo Grounds in New York to see Grange and the Bears play the Giants. Halas then took the team on a coast-to-coast tour of the country, playing games wherever he could find a team to

The great Chicago Bears teams of the 1940s included legendary running back Bronko Nagurski.

play them. This sparked even more interest in professional football.

Signing Grange for his Bears was only the first of Halas' many accomplishments. He was responsible for using the *T formation*, where three backs lined up behind the quarterback in what looks like a "T" shape. The backs and ends went in motion before the ball was snapped, allowing the Bears' quarterback many passing and running options. So devastating was this new strategy, the Bears practically owned the league before 1930. They won more games than any other team.

By 1933 Halas stopped playing in favor of coaching his Bears. 1933 was also the first year the NFL played in two divisions. The first post-season championship game featured the Eastern Division champs, the New York Giants, and the Western Division champs, the Chicago Bears. It was only fitting that this first championship game was won by the Bears, 23-21.

Halas coached some of the greatest teams ever seen in football. In 1940, the Bears ripped the overmatched Washington Redskins, 73-0. The following year, they did very much the same thing to the Giants, 37-9. Only after Halas and most of his magnificent team had left to join the war effort was it safe for other football teams to come out and play again. But once Halas returned from the war, the Bears' dominance was back.

By the 1960s Halas had become more than just another coach and owner; he had become The Coach. Nicknamed "Papa Bear," Halas always stood for excellence. Under his coaching, the Bears won league championships in seven seasons and division titles in four other years.

One of Papa Bear's best teams was saved for his last years as coach. The team featured Billy Wade at quarterback, the elusive Gale Sayers at halfback, the dauntless Mike Ditka at tight end, and the true Monster of the Midway, linebacker Dick Butkus. Few teams have been so exciting to watch.

Iron Mike

Even after Halas retired from coaching, he continued to be an active owner, overseeing the daily activities of the club. Before he died in 1988, he had the satisfaction of watching the coaching reins pass to one of his staunchest disciples, Mike Ditka. Ditka was a ball player of the old school—tough from the ground up. He had a 40-inch neck and a body like a fireplug. Nobody ever called "Iron Mike" Ditka a slouch on the field. When this future Hall of Famer became a coach, however, he inherited a slumbering Bears team. It was time to wake them up.

For starters, Ditka drafted players who would make ferocious Bears. His emphasis, like Halas before him, was on defense. Over the next three years, he managed to assemble one of the finest defensive teams ever seen. In the middle was team captain Mike Singletary and his partners in crime: Wilber Marshall, Otis Wilson, Gary Fencik, and Dave Duerson. The defensive front line was imposing, featuring Steve McMichaels, Dan Hampton, sack leader Richard Dent, and the monstrous William "The Fridge" Perry who weighed in at 330 pounds.

The Bears' offense was more than adequate. There was Walter Payton, nicknamed "Sweetness"—a kind and gentle soul off the field but a terror on it. With moves that would have made a cat envious, Payton tore up the NFL for 14 years. Before he retired in 1989, Payton would break most of the great Jim Brown's career rushing marks, including most yards rushing. The Bears even had the makings of a passing game, with world-class sprinter Willie Gault at wide end and Ken

Margerum at tight end.

The only thing the Bears lacked was a decent quarterback. That's when one of the strangest characters in football entered Bears' history: Jim McMahon. McMahon came out of BYU, where he had broken every NCAA passing record. He was as outspoken, rebellious, and just plain flakey as anyone who ever played football. But he was also a great leader. In no time the entire offensive line had become his best friend. And when he was played for the first time at the beginning of the 1982 season, McMahon immediately threw two touchdown passes that brought the Bears screaming back.

1985 was a dream season for the Bears. They were awesome. The defense crushed the opposition. It became routine to see the opponent's offense posting negative numbers for passing and rushing. In the middle of the season when the Bears were really humming, they skunked Detroit, Dallas, and Atlanta by a combined score of 104-3! Shutouts were normal. They went 18-1, and crushed the New England Patriots in Super Bowl XX, 46-10. For the '80s as a whole, they went .632, winning the NFC Central Division championship five times and placing 13 players in the Pro Bowl.

The Bears have continued their winning ways into the '90s under Iron Mike Ditka. And even without the flamboyant McMahon at quarterback, their defense and running game continue to make them perennial challengers for the league championship.

The Green Bay Packers of the 1960s had a real star at quarterback—Bart Starr. He was a cool passer who could get it in gear when necessary.

Lombardi And The New AFL

In 1958 the Green Bay Packers were getting nowhere fast. They had players with talent on their team, like wide receiver Max McGee, lineman Forrest Gregg, a tough rookie fullback named Jim Taylor, and 1956 Heisman Trophy winner Paul Hornung. What was missing, however, was a coach to blend these individual talents into a winning team. Green Bay decided on a bad-tempered assistant coach from the New York Giants named Vince Lombardi.

Lombardi was known as a tough coach and a tough negotiator. As part of his contract, he insisted on becoming the Packers' General Manager as well as coach, meaning that no one could override any of his decisions. He drilled his players without mercy. He introduced new plays that forced the team to think on the field. His rage made the players afraid to lose. The result of all his bullying and conditioning turned out to be victory.

In 1959 the Packers won game after game, but the turning point came when quarterback Lamar McHan was forced to the sidelines with a sore arm. The only other quarterback on the bench was a second-stringer named Bart Starr. They'd drafted Starr in the 17th round, and he had worked hard to become an accurate passer. Starr became the starting quarterback for the rest of the season. "The Pack" finished the year 7-5—their first winning season since 1947. Lombardi was selected Coach of the Year, and that was just the beginning.

1961 heralded the golden age of Packer football. Taylor and Hornung slashed through the line. Starr shook up the opponent's deep coverage with throws to McGee and Marv Fleming. Forrest Gregg led a defense that included Willie McGee and Ray Nitschke, among others. The Packers ruled the NFL. They came out on top after a solid 11-3 season, finishing off the Giants with a stomping 37-0 victory—their first championship since 1944.

The Packers were even more polished in 1962. Many fans still rate the '62 Packers as one of the greatest teams of all time. Bart Starr passed for 2,438 yards, with only nine interceptions. Jim Taylor, who enjoyed running through tacklers, had a record-setting 1,474 yards with 19 touchdowns. The Packer defense was the best in the NFL. The result was a sparkling 13-1 season and, once again, the Packers met the Giants in the NFL championship game and won.

In 1965, Lombardi acquired a new star: ace punter and kicker Don Chandler. Chandler led the league in scoring and helped move the Packers into the title game against Cleveland, which they wrapped up in convincing fashion, 23-13.

In 1966, Green Bay went 10-3 and beat Dallas in the last NFL championship game, 34-27. The following year, they went 12-2 for the season, beating out the Los Angeles Rams for a chance to play in the first Super Bowl, where they ran all over the Kansas City Chiefs, 35-10. The victory was classic Packers, with Hornung and Taylor running the defensive line ragged.

The Packers tried again the next year. Even without Jim Taylor and Paul Hornung, who had moved on to other teams, the Packers were good enough to go 9-4-1. They beat Los Angeles in the semifinals, 28-7, for the right to play in Super Bowl II where they met the upstart Oakland Raiders in the game still known as

Green Bay running back Donny Anderson (44) scores the Packer's fourth TD against Oakland in Super Bowl II. Although the Raiders lost, they would return victorious in future Super Bowls.

"The Ice Bowl." Fittingly, the game was decided on the last play when Bart Starr plunged into the end zone from the one-yard line for the final score, beating the Raiders 21-17.

    Super Bowl II was Vince Lombardi's final game as coach. He left the field on his players' shoulders. It was also the end of Green Bay's Golden Era. The Packers had won more consistently than any other team in pro football history, racking up six championships in eight years (1960-68), and four in a row (1964-68). No team had done it before, and no team has done it since. No team has been associated more closely with the word "dynasty" than the Green Bay Packers of the 1960s.

The Renegade Raiders

The time was the 1960s. Many NFL fans disliked the upstart American Football League, and no one except their fans liked the AFL's most notorious team: the Oakland Raiders. The team wore black and silver uniforms, were sore losers, and did the most terrible things to their opponents—mostly beating them. Under coaches Al Davis, John Madden, and Tom Flores, this bunch of misfits made the AFL—now the American Football Conference (AFC)—a respectable force.

The Oakland Raiders were the last AFL team to be organized in 1960, and so they got everyone else's castaways. Worse yet, they didn't even have a home. The owners were still trying to find a stadium. Their first three years the Raiders went 6-8, 2-12, and 1-13. Hardly a good beginning. But the person who turned the franchise into a winner was the man hired as coach for the 1963 season: Al Davis.

Davis' coaching style was anything but Lombardi or Halas. Davis preferred to be friends with his players—players who either didn't fit in or didn't get along with their previous teams. There was quarterback Darryl Lamonica, running backs Cotton Davidson and Bo Robertson, lineman Willie Brown, wide end Fred Biletnikoff, and Ben Davidson. They were a scary crew, even though some of them were getting old, like George Blanda—a 19-year veteran quarterback and kicker.

Davis began by emphasizing the importance of poise and pride on his team. He knitted this odd bunch into a solid team. Most fans didn't expect much in those first seasons. They were in for a surprise.

The persistence of Al Davis, one-time coach and present owner of the Los Angeles Raiders, led his upstart West Coast team to four AFC championships and three Super Bowl wins.

1964 would mark the last year the Oakland Raiders ever had a losing season. In 1967, they recorded a 13-1 season, defeated the Houston Oilers for the AFL championship, and were suddenly in Super Bowl II. The boys in black and silver had to fight uphill against the defending champs, Green Bay, losing 33-14.

Oakland repeated as Western Division champs not once, not twice, but seven times. Except for 1971, the Raiders led their division every year through 1975,

17

compiling a record of 115 wins, 42 losses, and 11 ties. Their average of .732 was the best of any pro team! But despite these triumphs, Oakland had not yet won the big one, the Super Bowl.

    1976 was a different story. John Madden was now coach. The Raiders swept through the regular season with a 13-1 mark, then went into the Conference final against Pittsburgh and drubbed them, 24-7. In the Super Bowl, they faced Fran Tarkenton and the Minnesota Vikings. It was the Vikings' fourth Super Bowl and they wanted it badly. But there is an inevitability to football. The elements that had made the Raiders so unbeatable during the season made them equally unbeatable against the Vikings. The Raiders dismantled the Vikings and walked away with the Super Bowl, 32-14.

    The next two years were a letdown. In 1978 the Raiders finished 9-7 and didn't make the playoffs for only the second time in 12 years. Madden retired. Tom Flores, the Raiders first quarterback, became coach. But he couldn't help the Raiders in '79. Quarterback Kenny Stabler was getting older. The young superstar they'd drafted from BYU, Marc Wilson, was too inexperienced. Davis made a surprising decision by drafting a third quarterback: Heisman Trophy winner Jim Plunkett.

    From the moment Plunkett stepped on the field in 1980, the Raiders had a magic touch. They didn't do particularly well in the regular season, but well enough to qualify for a wild-card spot. They made the most of it. First they beat Cleveland 14-12 in the wild-card game, then eliminated the Chargers 34-27 in the conference championship. Next came the Super Bowl and Philadelphia. It was no surprise when Plunkett engineered a brilliant day of passing, landing the MVP award for himself and the Lombardi Award for the team. The final score was Raiders 27, Eagles 10.

Jim Plunkett captained the Raiders in Super Bowls XV and XVIII—and was named Most Valuable Player in XV.

In 1982 the Raiders moved to Los Angeles, becoming the L.A. Raiders. After a fine 12-4 record in 1983, they beat both Pittsburgh and Seattle behind the savage defense of Lyle Alzado and the rest of the crew. Meanwhile, Jim Plunkett was unstoppable. Los Angeles never let up on the Redskins in Super Bowl XVIII. John Riggins was held to only 64 yards in 26 carries, and the Redskins suffered a one-sided loss, 38-9. For the third time the Raiders had won the Super Bowl, joining the ranks of the football dynasties.

Dave Meggett is the latest star on a New York Giants team that has won two Super Bowls (XXI and XXV).

From New York To Dallas

New York seems to be a city of dynasties. In baseball, the Yankees dynasty has never been equaled. In basketball, the Knicks have been a powerful force. In football, the team to reckon with has always been the Giants. It should come as no surprise then that the Giants have had three dynasty teams. The first came in the 1930s, the second in the 1950s, the third in the 1980s.

The first great Giants team was run by Steve Owen, who became head coach in 1934. The team won their first championship that same year, and another in 1938 to go along with division titles in 1941, 1944, and 1946. The great offensive threat in those years was "Fabulous Frankie" Filchock, a master at the run-pass option.

Dynasty Trivia

Q: Name the first team to win back-to-back Super Bowls.
A: The Green Bay Packers (I and II).

Q: Name the head coach who has been to the Super Bowl more than any other.
A: Don Shula, with six appearances.

Q: Name the two championship football teams that have each lost in four Super Bowl appearances.
A: The Minnesota Vikings (IV, VIII, IX, and XI) and the Denver Broncos (XII, XXI, XXII, XXIV) have yet to win the Super Bowl.

Hall of Famer and future sports broadcaster Frank Gifford was part of a strong Giants offense in the late 1950s.

With Filchock scoring points and the Giants' line mowing down opponents, they were rarely out of contention for the league championship.

But by the late 1940s, the Giants were just another team. Owner Tim Mara replaced Owen with former Giant lineman Jim Lee Howell, who believed in finding good assistants for his coaching staff, like Vince Lombardi, Tom Landry, and Dick Nolan. He also traded for a third-year pro from USC named Frank Gifford. Gifford was a good safety, a good receiver, an accurate passer, a pretty fair rusher, and a reliable place kicker.

In other words, Gifford was a multiple threat—one of the finest all-purpose players in pro football history. Working with quarterback Charley Conerly (named Rookie of the Year in 1948), the Giants once again had an effective offense. And the New York defense with the legendary Sam Huff was just plain mean. They suffocated opponents, ran through their lines, batted away all attempts to pass, and crushed the run.

In 1956 the Giants took this team into the NFL finals against the favored Bears. The turf was frozen. The Giants appeared in sneakers and proceeded to romp over the Bears, winning by a lopsided 47-7. Two years later, the Giants were back again in the championship game against Johnny Unitas and the Baltimore Colts. In one of pro football's most famous games, the Giants lost in overtime, 23-17. In 1963, the 10-3 Giants met the Bears in the championship finals and lost a heartbreaker 14-10 when superstar Y.A. Tittle was injured in the third quarter.

Recent Success

After 1963, the Giants slept for a long time. While never the worst team in the league, they were reduced to also-rans. But fame wasn't finished with the Giants. Phil Simms was drafted in 1979. Then, in 1981, their number one draft choice was Lawrence Taylor, perhaps the most gifted defensive player in history. Coached expertly by defensive coordinator Bill Parcells, the Giants once again became the bullies of the NFL. In 1981, they cruised into the Super Bowl for the first time, but lost to San Francisco.

Bill Parcells took over as coach in 1982, but with Phil Simms on the injured list, the Giants finished in last place. The New York fans grumbled, but Parcells was undaunted. He knew he could win. In 1984 the Giants went to the Super Bowl once again, and once again they lost to the 49ers. But it wasn't as easy for San Francisco this time. Taylor and the defense were tougher, and the offense was more mature but still missing a few pieces.

The missing pieces turned out to be speedy running back Joe Morris, fullback Ottis Anderson, and tight end Mark Bavaro. With these three players rounding out the offense, the Giants finally emerged as number one.

In 1986 it wasn't even a contest. The Giants were the best team from start to finish. While the Taylor-led defense stuffed opposing teams, Phil Simms led a smooth, efficient attack that ground up yardage and opponents with machine-like accuracy. The Giants simply stampeded over their rivals. When the smoke cleared, it was the Denver Broncos against the Giants in the Super Bowl. This time, Simms, Bavaro, Taylor, and company made no bones about it. They crushed the hapless Broncos 39-20 and secured their first Super Bowl ring.

In 1990 the Giants returned, this time with Jeff Hostetler at quarterback. Compiling a 13-3 record on their way to reclaiming Super Bowl XXVI, they first eliminated the 49ers in one of the most exciting divisional championship games on record, then beat Jim Kelly and the Buffalo Bills in heart-stopping fashion, 20-19.

America's Team

In 1960 the NFL refused to grant a new franchise to LaMar Hunt, a Texas billionaire. In typical Texas style, Hunt had decided to start his own team, the Dallas Texans, and his own league. Finally the NFL gave in and the Dallas Cowboys were born.

New coach Tom Landry had to scrape the bottom of the football barrels to find enough talent to fill his

The great Tony Dorsett of the Dallas Cowboys racked up more yardage than any other player except Walter Payton.

starting roster. Before coming to Dallas, he had invented the 4-3 defense (four linemen and three linebackers), which was to become the defense of choice for the entire NFL. Now, as coach of an under-talented team, Landry had to invent a way of overcoming his own 4-3 defense. The result was a playbook so large and so complex that no other team could figure it out.

    Results were not immediate. In their first season, the Cowboys didn't win a single game, and there were several more losing seasons. But in 1966 they went 10-3 with quarterbacks Don Meredith and Craig Morton and a "Doomsday Defense" that sacked opposing quarterbacks 60 times. They stomped the Atlanta Falcons 47-14, humiliated the Philadelphia Eagles 56-7,

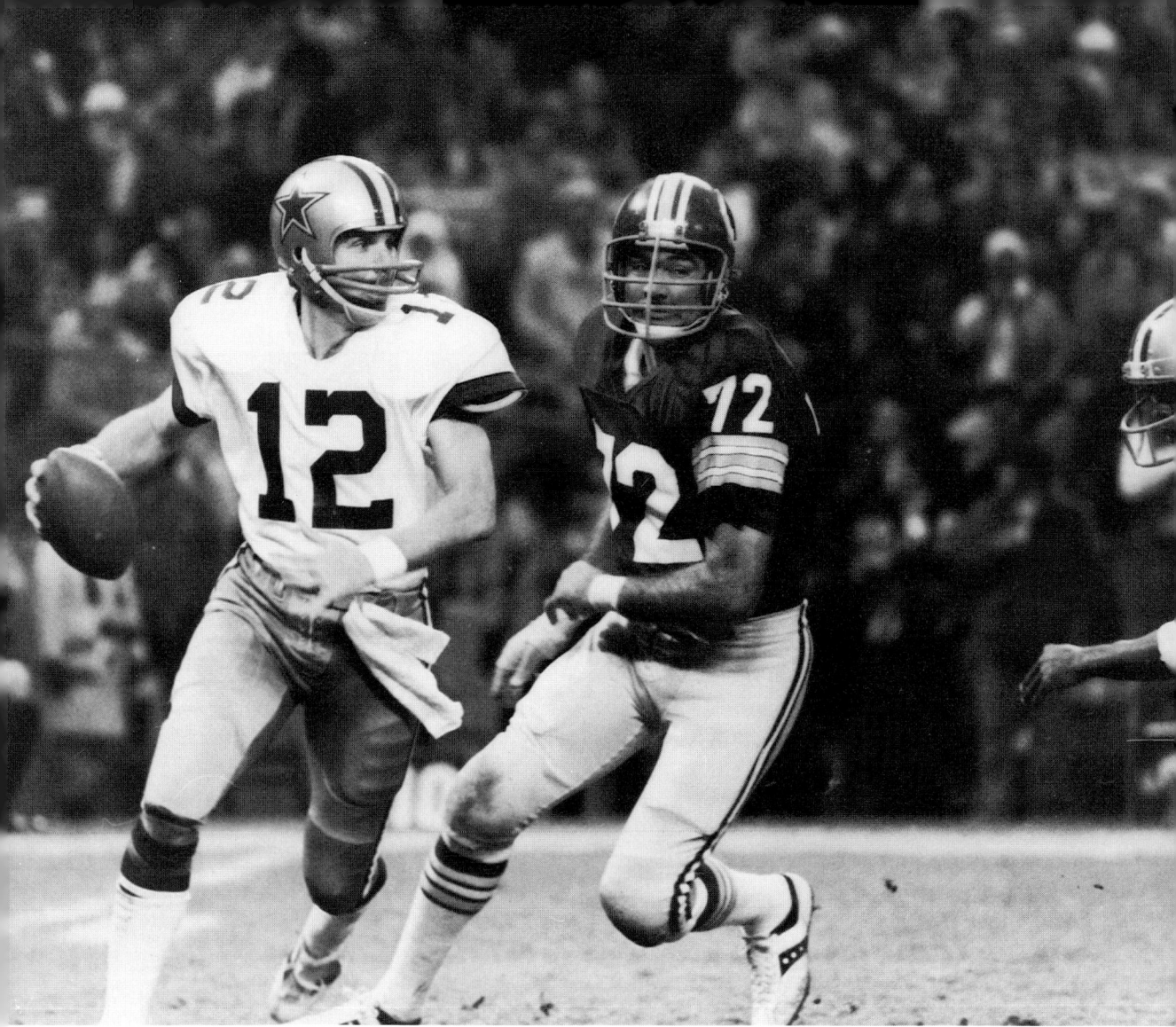

Heisman Trophy winner Roger Staubach (left) led two Cowboy teams to Super Bowl victories.

and landed themselves in the NFL championship game. Too bad it had to be against the Green Bay Packers, who were still in a league by themselves. Dallas lost 34-27.

Things finally fell into place in 1971 when Coach Landry finally settled on Heisman Trophy winner Roger Staubach as his full-time quarterback. Staubach responded by assembling the best statistics for any NFC quarterback and leading the Cowboys to an 11-3 mark. In the playoffs, Dallas continued their domination by beating the Vikings and the 49ers. In Super Bowl VI

Dallas dumped the Miami Dolphins, 24-3.

For the next five years, the Cowboys were one of the most successful franchises and perhaps the most talented in all of football. Their popularity made them "America's Team" to millions of television watchers. With Staubach at quarterback and a succession of good running backs and strong linemen, Dallas was never far out of the hunt for the Super Bowl.

After a disappointing season in 1976, where they compiled a fine 11-3 record but lost 14-12 in the first playoff to L.A., the Cowboys looked forward to redeeming themselves in 1977. They played the '77 season like men possessed, finishing with a 12-2 record. Sweeping through the playoff opposition, they beat Chicago 37-7 and the Vikings 23-6. In Super Bowl XII they met the Denver Broncos and the "Orange Crush" defense. The Denver fans were wild with excitement, but Roger Staubach soon cooled them down with pinpoint passes. When it was all over, the Cowboys had tamed the Broncos for their second Super Bowl ring, 27-10. The next year they made another Super Bowl appearance, but lost to Pittsburgh, 35-31.

The Cowboys never rose to that same level of excellence again. They were a good team, at least until Roger Staubach retired in 1982, but never again a great team. The crown of America's favorite team was inevitably passed on.

Dolphins receiver Marlin Briscoe (86) hauls in a pass from Hall of Fame quarterback Bob Griese on the Minnesota Vikings' one-yard line.

The Dolphins And The Steelers

For years the Miami Dolphins were just another expansion team going nowhere in the AFL. They had some good draft picks: Bob Griese, Larry Csonka, Jim Kiick, and Dick Anderson. They got Nick Buoniconti and Mercury Morris in trades. But what the Dolphins needed, however, was a good coach. Lucky for them they hired Don Shula.

Shula had just led the Baltimore Colts to Super Bowl III. Upon arriving in Miami, he announced that he wasn't a miracle-worker, then proceeded to work miracles. He helped train wide receiver Paul Warfield into a speedy threat. He hired a European soccer player named Garo Yepremian to be his field-goal kicker. Shula developed a playbook heavy on exciting plays. The result was a 10-4 season in 1970, including six wins in a row. In 1971, he watched his Dolphins improve to 10-3-1. They went into the AFC championship game against the Kansas City Chiefs as underdogs, and in the longest game ever played—almost five full quarters—the Dolphins finally prevailed, 27-24. But in Super Bowl VI, Shula was disappointed as the Cowboys beat Miami 27-6.

The Dolphins were too good to be denied. The next year, 1972, they were back. Shula had taken out quarterback insurance by acquiring Earl Morrall from the Colts. At age 38 he was one of the oldest players in pro football. The insurance paid off, however, when Griese broke his ankle in the fifth game. Miami fans silently kissed their 4-0 start goodbye, along with any chance of a winning season or a Super Bowl ring. But Earl Morrall was made of special stuff, and 1972 turned out to be a special year for the Dolphins and for NFL history.

Morrall led the Dolphins through a rigorous schedule winning all nine remaining games and finishing 14-0. It was the first time since 1942 that any pro team had won all eleven regular season games.

The first playoff game pitted Miami against the wild-card Browns, and for most of the game it was nip and tuck. But in the fourth quarter, with just minutes remaining, Morrall led the Dolphins on an 80-yard drive in just seven plays. The final score was 20-14. Then they beat the Steelers in the AFC title game, 21-17. Now the record stood at 16-0. Only Super Bowl VII stood in the way of a perfect season.

Bob Griese was back for the finale against the Washington Redskins. At half time the score was 14-0 Dolphins—the only points Miami would get that day, and the only points they would need. Manny Fernandez kept on sacking Redskin quarterback Billy Kilmer and the defense never gave the Washington offense a break. The final score was 14-7, and Miami had a perfect 17-0 record.

Miami had another great year in 1973, finishing 12-2. It was Shula's fondest hope to follow in the footsteps of his hero, Vince Lombardi, by leading his team to back-to-back championships. This he did, beating the Minnesota Vikings in the Super Bowl. The Dolphins had gone 32-2, including two Super Bowl victories, establishing themselves as one of the true dynasties in the history of NFL football.

The Steel Curtain

When people discuss the truly great NFL teams, it usually comes down to three: the Packers, the 49ers, and the Pittsburgh Steelers. The Steelers were born in 1933, and throughout their first four decades, they had a lot of winning seasons but never won a championship.

In 1968 the Steelers took their first step toward greatness. Owner Art Rooney found the coach he had been looking for: Chuck Noll. When Rooney hired Noll, he asked him, "Are you aware that historically this is a city of losers?" Noll responded: "Then we'll just have to change history."

He was as good as his word. Noll believed in young blood and the college draft. He felt that trading only brought another team's problem players into a ball club. And he believed in defense.

In 1969, Noll picked defensive tackle Joe Greene from North Texas State as his No. 1 draft choice. From Arkansas AM&N he drafted defensive end L.C. Greenwood, and from Oklahoma State he got offensive tackle Jon Kolb. But that wasn't enough, and the 1969 season was a 1-13 flop. The one good thing it did for the club, however, was to allow them another chance at high draft choices. In 1970 Noll took full advantage of this when he drafted college football's best quarterback at the time, Terry Bradshaw. The kid had a bazooka for an arm and a body that could take a lot of pounding. In 1972 Noll drafted Franco Harris. Later he added receivers Lynn Swann and John Stallworth, as well as linebackers Jack Lambert and Jack Ham. The Steelers were ready.

The fans called their defense "The Steel Curtain." Nothing got by them. In 1974 the Steelers went 10-3, and in the AFC championship game they picked off two Kenny Stabler passes. It had taken Art Rooney 41 years to see his team in a championship game, but suddenly

In the 1970s, Terry Bradshaw played for the Pittsburgh Steelers and became the NFL's top quarterback.

Steelers coach Chuck Noll put together the awesome Steel Curtain defense and a remarkable running and passing game to bring the city of Pittsburgh four Super Bowl wins.

the Steelers were in Super Bowl IX against the Vikings. Franco Harris ran 158 yards on 34 plays. The Curtain rang down on Viking quarterback Fran Tarkenton, whose team was limited to only 17 yards rushing! The final score was 17-7.

    The Steelers were just getting started. The next year, Terry Bradshaw came into his own as a starting quarterback. Super Bowl IX had built his confidence, and now with Stallworth and Swann as willing targets,

Franco Harris played for the Steelers dynasty and earned his place in the record books with the fourth-best rushing record in NFL history.

the Steelers thoroughly dominated the opposition. They finished with a 12-2 mark, and made it to Super Bowl X. Now the question was, could they do something only done by two other teams in NFL history—win back-to-back Super Bowls? The Dallas Cowboys didn't lie down for Pittsburgh, but they couldn't score either. The Steel Curtain suffocated them. Pittsburgh swept by Dallas, 21-10.

For several seasons after that, the Steelers misfired. In 1976, despite injuries to Bradshaw, Swann, and Harris, the Steelers came within one game of going to their third straight Super Bowl. But the 1978 season was different. They wound up with a 14-2 record, best in the NFL. Once more, the two-time Super Bowl champions faced Dallas in Super Bowl XIII. And once more they beat the Cowboys, 35-31.

Pittsburgh pounded its way through the 1979 season with a 12-4 record. The legendary Steel Curtain never had a better season. The finale came on January 20, 1980, when the Steelers took on the L.A. Rams in California's famous Rose Bowl before a record-breaking crowd of 103,000. The Rams stayed tough for much of the game, even managing a 19-17 lead at one point. But when the final whistle blew, the Steelers had annihilated the Rams, 35-19. It was the Steelers' fourth Super Bowl. They had won back-to-back Super Bowls twice. From then on, all NFL teams would be measured against the greatness of the Pittsburgh Steelers.

Redskins quarterback Mark Rypien was the obvious choice for MVP in Washington's win in Super Bowl XXVI.

Dynasties Of The Eighties

The Washington Redskins were always a good team and frequently a great one. Unlike many teams built on a solid core of young talent, the Redskins seemed to specialize in recycled players and old pros so that the team never seemed to get any younger. But they frequently got better. They had enjoyed championship years in the 1930s and '40s with Hall of Fame quarterback Sammy Baugh, but their real glory years were still ahead of them.

In the 1970s, the Redskins posted nine consecutive seasons with better than .500. By 1980 they had assembled a team that featured quarterback Joe Theismann, fullback John Riggins, linemen Mark May and Russ Grimm, receivers Alvin Garrett and Charlie Brown, and Art Monk and Rick Walker at tight end. The new-look Redskins took a year to gel, winning the last eight games of the 1981 season and barely finishing out of the playoffs. But 1982 was a different story. After a winning season, the Redskins plowed into the playoffs, taming the Lions and sinking the Vikings. Then it was on to Super Bowl XVII for a meeting with Miami. The Dolphins had won back-to-back Super Bowls, but the Redskins stifled them at every turn. The final score was 20-17, and the team from Washington had won it all.

In 1987 Coach Joe Gibbs tried back-up quarterback Doug Williams. While Williams wasn't the first black quarterback in the league (there had been 11 before him), he was certainly the most visible. He'd been knocking around the NFL for 10 years, knocking down racial barriers in the process. Rumors about him said he was a streaky passer and inconsistent playmaker. But in 1987, Williams was simply the best. Under his leadership, the Redskins returned to top form, compiling an 11-4 record and sweeping into the playoffs. In Super Bowl XXII, the Redskins crushed the hapless Broncos, 42-10. Doug Williams was named the Super Bowl MVP, and it was the second Lombardi Trophy for the Redskins.

Two Super Bowl championships would have been enough for most teams, but the Redskins were exceptional. There was too much talent on this team. In 1991, quarterback Mark Rypien proved that he was not only agile in the backfield but a first-rate passer. Once again Coach Gibbs and company were up to their old tricks, going 14-2 for the season—including a string of eight straight wins. Super Bowl XXVI marked a fitting end to the season as the Redskins drubbed the Buffalo Bills 37-24. It was their third Super Bowl victory, making them a true dynasty.

Dynasty By The Bay

The greatest team of the 1980s was the San Francisco 49ers. San Francisco had always been an interesting team, but never a contender. That changed in 1978 when owner Eddy DeBartolo hired the head coach at Stanford University, Bill Walsh. Walsh brought with him a fine coaching mind. He picked carefully among the available talent in the '79 draft.

San Francisco needed a new quarterback, but quarterbacks were in short supply in the 1979 draft and most pro teams didn't really know what to look for. It wasn't until the 82nd pick that Walsh and DeBartolo finally claimed a quarterback from Notre Dame. All 28 teams had passed over Joe Montana, not once, but three

Joe Montana's cool skill as San Francisco's quarterback helped make the 49ers four-time Super Bowl champions.

Jerry Rice completes another pass pattern. His ability has made him one of the game's all-time great receivers.

times. It was an interesting beginning for the man who would become the greatest quarterback of all time. Montana was only the first of many good picks.

There was Roger Craig, Russ Francis, Dwight Clark, Ronnie Lott, Eric Wright, and Keena Turner. And there was wide receiver Jerry Rice. Rice and Montana went together like pork and beans. If Montana became the game's greatest quarterback, then Jerry Rice was surely among the greatest wide receivers.

Once the players were in place, Walsh trained them, teaching them plays that no one else in the league would ever think of using. He also disciplined them to think while they were out on the field. Rarely, if ever, has a team been smarter than the 49ers.

The 49ers' advance into football legend began in 1981, when they finished with a highly respectable 13-3. As they had done all season, they dispatched the Giants 38-24 and the Cowboys 28-27, using a combination of Montana passes and Roger Craig runs. Meanwhile, the 49er defense held whenever necessary. In their first Super Bowl, San Francisco finished off the Bengals 26-21 with Joe Montana winning MVP. It would be only the first of several big wins for the 49ers and their faithful fans.

In 1984 the 49ers improved to a sparkling 15-1, clearly the best team in the league. In Super Bowl XVI they demolished the Dolphins 38-16 for their second Lombardi trophy. Then for three years San Francisco didn't make the Super Bowl. They continued to do well, racking up more than ten wins in each year, but they couldn't make it past the playoffs. But in 1988 the 49ers finished 10-6, and were once more Super Bowl bound.

The Cincinnati Bengals and Boomer Esiason proved unexpectedly tough in Super Bowl XXIII. They took the game into the fourth quarter, but an incredible last-minute drive by Montana pulled it out, 20-16. This victory was Coach Walsh's last. He retired, leaving the job to his chief disciple, George Siefert.

Did Walsh's retirement mean the end of the San Francisco dynasty? Not at all. In 1989, the team went 14-2—again the best record in football. Every aspect of their game was polished. The offensive line protected Montana. Roger Craig broke the middle of the line, and the defense stopped the opponents cold. Super Bowl XXIV was more of a clinic than a real football game as San Francisco humiliated the Denver Broncos, 55-10.

At the end of the 1989 season no one could doubt that the 49ers were the greatest team of the decade. They had won four Super Bowls in eight years, and created a new style of high-tech football. The sport will never be the same because of the San Francisco 49ers.

NFL-NFC Championship Games

Season	Winner	Score	Loser
1933	Chicago Bears	23-21	New York
1934	New York	30-13	Chicago Bears
1935	Detroit	26-7	New York
1936	Green Bay	21-6	Boston Redskins
1937	Washington Redskins	28-21	Chicago Bears
1938	New York	23-17	Green Bay
1939	Green Bay	27-0	New York
1940	Chicago Bears	73-0	Washington
1941	Chicago Bears	37-9	New York
1942	Washington	14-6	Chicago Bears
1943	Chicago Bears	41-21	Washington
1944	Green Bay	14-7	New York
1945	Cleveland Rams	15-14	Washington
1946	Chicago Bears	24-14	New York
1947	Chicago Cards	28-21	Philadelphia
1948	Philadelphia	7-0	Chicago Cards
1949	Philadelphia	14-0	Los Angeles
1950	Cleveland Browns	30-28	Los Angeles
1951	Los Angeles	24-17	Cleveland
1952	Detroit	17-7	Cleveland
1953	Detroit	17-16	Cleveland
1954	Cleveland	56-10	Detroit
1955	Cleveland	38-14	Los Angeles
1956	New York	47-7	Chicago Bears
1957	Detroit	59-14	Cleveland
1958	Baltimore	23-17	New York
1959	Baltimore	31-16	New York

NFL-NFC Championship Games

Season	Winner	Score	Loser
1960	Philadelphia	17-13	Green Bay
1961	Green Bay	37-0	New York
1962	Green Bay	16-7	New York
1963	Chicago	14-10	New York
1964	Cleveland	27-0	Baltimore
1965	Green Bay	23-12	Cleveland
1966	Green Bay	34-27	Dallas
1967	Green Bay	21-17	Dallas
1968	Baltimore	34-0	Cleveland
1969	Minnesota	27-7	Cleveland
1970	Dallas	17-10	San Francisco
1971	Dallas	14-3	San Francisco
1972	Washington	26-3	Dallas
1973	Minnesota	27-10	Dallas
1974	Minnesota	14-10	Los Angeles
1975	Dallas	37-7	Los Angeles
1976	Minnesota	24-13	Los Angeles
1977	Dallas	23-6	Minnesota
1978	Dallas	28-0	Los Angeles
1979	Los Angeles	9-0	Tampa Bay
1980	Philadelphia	20-7	Dallas
1981	San Francisco	28-27	Dallas
1982	Washington	31-17	Dallas
1983	Washington	24-21	San Francisco
1984	San Francisco	23-0	Chicago
1985	Chicago	24-0	Los Angeles
1986	New York	17-0	Washington
1987	Washington	17-10	Minnesota
1988	San Francisco	28-3	Chicago
1989	San Francisco	30-3	Los Angeles
1990	New York	15-13	San Francisco
1991	Washington	41-10	Detroit

AFL-AFC Championship Games

Season	Winner	Score	Loser
1960	Houston	24-16	LA Chargers
1961	Houston	10-3	SD Chargers
1962	Dallas	20-17	Houston
1963	San Diego	51-10	Boston Patriots
1964	Buffalo	20-7	San Diego
1965	Buffalo	23-0	San Diego
1966	Kansas City	31-7	Buffalo
1967	Oakland	40-7	Houston
1968	New York Jets	27-23	Oakland
1969	Kansas City	17-7	Oakland
1970	Baltimore	27-17	Oakland
1971	Miami	21-0	Baltimore
1972	Miami	21-17	Pittsburgh
1973	Miami	27-10	Oakland
1974	Pittsburgh	24-13	Oakland
1975	Pittsburgh	16-10	Oakland
1976	Oakland	24-7	Pittsburgh
1977	Denver	20-17	Oakland
1978	Pittsburgh	34-5	Houston
1979	Pittsburgh	27-13	Houston
1980	Oakland	34-27	San Diego
1981	Cincinnati	27-7	San Diego
1982	Miami	14-0	NY Jets
1983	LA Raiders	30-14	Seattle
1984	Miami	45-28	Pittsburgh
1985	New England Patriots	31-14	Miami
1986	Denver	23-20	Cleveland
1987	Denver	38-33	Cleveland
1988	Cincinnati	21-10	Buffalo
1989	Denver	37-21	Cleveland
1990	Buffalo	51-3	LA Raiders
1991	Buffalo	10-7	Denver

Glossary

AFC. American Football Conference, formerly the American Football League (AFL).

AFL. American Football League, now the American Football Conference (AFC).

DRAFT. A method by which pro football teams pick and choose the top athletes from college teams. The pro teams with the previous season's worst records get the top picks.

DYNASTY. A team that dominates its sport year after year.

FIELD GOAL. A three-point play made by kicking the football through the other team's goal posts or "uprights."

GRIDIRON. The football field.

NFC. National Football Conference.

NFL. National Football League, comprised of the American Football Conference (AFC) and the National Football Conference (NFC).

QUARTERBACK SNEAK. A play where the quarterback takes the snap and immediately follows the center forward past the line of scrimmage for short yardage.

ROOKIE. A first-year player in any pro sport.

T FORMATION. An offensive set-up where the backs line up behind the quarterback, forming a letter "T" behind the front line.

TOUCHDOWN. The six-point play made by carrying or catching the football beyond the opposing team's goal line and into their end zone.

Picture Credits

ALLSPORT USA: 20 (Stephen Dunn); 25, 34 (Rick Stewart); 36, 40 (Mike Powell); 39 (Otto Greule, Jr.)
The Bettman Archive: 15, 28, 32
NFL Properties: 4
Wide World Photos: 8, 12, 17, 19, 22, 26, 33

Bibliography

Benagh, Jim. *Football: Startling Stories Behind the Records.* New York: Sterling, 1986.

Hollander, Zander. *The Complete Handbook of Pro Football.* New York: Signet, 1991.

Madden, John. *John Madden's Pro Football Annual, 1991.* New York: Random House, 1991.

McMahon, Jim with Bob Verdi. *McMahon!* New York: Warner Books, 1988.

Meserole, Mike, ed. *The 1992 Information Please Sports Almanac.* Boston: Houghton Mifflin, 1992.

Neft, David S. and Richard M. Cohen. *The Sports Encyclopedia: Pro Football.* New York: St. Martin's Press, 1985.

Porter, David L. *Biographical Dictionary of American Sports: Football.* New York: Greenwood Press, 1987.

Riffenburgh, Beau and Bill Barron. *The Official NFL Encyclopedia.* New York: New American Library, 1986.

Taylor, Lawrence. *LT: Living on the Edge.* New York: Times Books, 1989.

Trope, Mike and Steve Delsohn. *Necessary Roughness.* New York: Contemporary Books, 1989.

Index

American Football League (AFL), 16

Baltimore Colts, 23, 29
Blanda, George, 16
Bradshaw, Terry, 31-35
Brown, Jim, 10
Butkus, Dick, 10

Chandler, Don, 14
Chicago Bears, 7-11, 23, 27
Cleveland Browns, 14, 18, 30
Craig, Roger, 40-41

Dallas Cowboys, 14, 24-27, 29, 35, 41
Davis, Al, 16-19
Denver Broncos, 6, 21, 24, 27, 38
Ditka, Mike, 10-11
Dorsett, Tony, 25

Flores, Tom, 16, 18
Fouts, Dan, 5-6

Gibbs, Joe, 37-38
Gifford, Frank, 22-23
Grange, Red, 7-9
Green Bay Packers, 13-16, 17, 21, 26, 31
Gregg, Forrest, 13, 14

Halas, George, 4, 7-10, 16
Harris, Franco, 31-35
Hornung, Paul, 13, 14

Landry, Tom, 22, 24-27
Largent, Steve, 6
Lombardi, Vince, 4, 13-16, 22, 30
Los Angeles Raiders
  see Oakland-L.A. Raiders
Los Angeles Rams, 14, 27, 35

Madden, John, 16, 18
McGee, Max, 13, 14
McMahon, Jim, 11
Meggett, Dave, 20
Miami Dolphins, 21, 27, 29-30, 41

Montana, Joe, 38-41
Morrall, Earl, 29-30

Nagurski, Bronko, 8
New York Giants, 9, 13, 14, 21-24
Noll, Chuck, 31, 33

Oakland-L.A. Raiders, 14-15, 16-19

Parcells, Bill, 23-24
Payton, Walter, 10, 25
Philadelphia Eagles, 18, 25
Pittsburgh Steelers, 19, 31-35
Plunkett, Jim, 18-19

Rice, Jerry, 40-41
Rypien, Mark, 36, 38

San Diego Chargers, 5-6
San Francisco 49ers, 31, 38-41
Sayers, Gale, 9
Shula, Don, 21, 29-30
Simms, Phil, 23-24
Singletary, Mike, 10
Starr, Bart, 12, 13-16
Staubach, Roger, 26-27

T formation, 9
Tarkenton, Fran, 18, 33
Taylor, Jim, 13, 14
Taylor, Lawrence, 23-24

Walsh, Bill, 38-41
Washington Redskins, 9, 19, 30, 37-38
Williams, Doug, 37-38